ANIMAL RECORDS

Humans can do some great things. They can travel at immense speeds, lift heavy weights and fly great distances. For these things, of course, they need machines they have invented and built. Animals, too, can reach very high speeds, fly thousands of miles or lift many times their own weight; indeed, animals hold some pretty incredible records. What's more, animals have no technical achievements to their name: they must make do with what nature has given them—which makes their performance all the more extraordinary. This book will tell you about some amazing things animals can do.

THE WORLD'S FASTEST ANIMALS

Let's start in high gear. Some of the animals you will read about are a match for a super-fast sports car. We're about to hold a great race that will show us, for sure, which creature is the world's fastest.

❋ CHEETAH

A beast of prey, the cheetah would be happy to see some of its rivals in today's competition on the menu. We must hope that the race will end with the full number of competitors. A cheetah reaches speeds of up to **75 mph**—making it as quick as a car driving on a highway.

❋ RACEHORSE

A racehorse is bred and trained to run fast. It has 252 bones in a huge, muscular body that weighs **1,300 pounds**. Horses can reach speeds of **35 mph**.

❋ BROWN HARE

Although it mainly inhabits fields and the edges of forests in Europe, the brown hare can also be found in Asia and elsewhere. It feeds on herbs and buds and tends to travel at around **25 mph**. In an emergency, though, it can run almost twice as fast.

CATEGORY:
RUNNING

✳ OSTRICH

The flightless ostrich is the world's largest living bird and quickest creature on two legs. It lives in Africa. Its typical speed is **35 mph**, although it can briefly maintain a speed of **55 mph**.

✳ PRONGHORN

The pronghorn, which lives in North America, is aptly named: its horns are shaped like prongs. One of the world's fastest mammals, it can reach a speed of **50–55 mph** and maintain it for many miles. The pronghorn is a great long-distance athlete.

✳ FASTEST HUMAN

The fastest recorded speed achieved by a human is **27.79 mph**. This record is held by Jamaican athlete Usain Bolt, whose specialty was the 100-meter sprint. Shortly, we will see how Bolt's achievement compares with those of our planet's fastest creatures.

And the first to reach the finish line is ... the cheetah!

RECORD-BREAKING RUNNERS

1 CHEETAH
75 mph

2  OSTRICH
55 mph

3 PRONGHORN
50–55 mph

4 HORSE
35 mph

5 HARE
25–50 mph

6  FASTEST HUMAN
27.79 mph

FLYERS

Our next race will be in flying. Although speedy animals can compete with cars and bikes on land, they are no match for human flying machines, of course. Even so, some animals are very impressive high-speed aviators.

The common swift lives in Europe and migrates to Africa in winter. Though a small bird, it is a record holder in many categories. It can fly for several months without stopping. But where does it sleep? In flight, of course! While one half of its brain sleeps, the other controls the flight. In this way, it flies almost **125,000 miles** per year. On a dive, it can reach speeds of over **125 mph**.

※ HORSEFLY

For humans, the horsefly is a pest with a painful bite. But you would struggle to find a more agile flyer. It does things in the air that aeronautical acrobats do, at speeds approaching **95 mph**.

The race ended as we expected. The winner is the peregrine falcon.

CATEGORY:

FLYING

2

1

3

❋ SPARROW

This small bird—only a little over 4 in long—is found all over the world. Despite its small size and roundness, it can reach relatively high speeds of over **30 mph**.

❋ PEREGRINE FALCON

This flyer, too, is found in most of the world. Thanks to its long, pointed wings, it can dive at a speed of over **185 mph**—making it not only the fastest bird but also the fastest of all animals on our planet.

RECORD-BREAKING FLYERS

1

FALCON
185 mph

2

SWIFT
125 mph

3

HORSEFLY
95 mph

4

SPARROW
30 mph

SWIMMERS

Let's move over to the pool, where the swimming race is about to start. There are many record holders among sea creatures, too. Allow us to introduce the best of them.

✱ SWORDFISH

Although this racer weighs **1,400 lbs**, it zooms through the water at **60 mph**. Like the sailfish, it uses its sword when hunting, waving it about in a school of sardines before feeding on the ones it has injured. It can leap high above the water.

✱ ORCA

People used to believe that orca attacked humans, hence its other name—killer whale. But now we know that our first starter isn't a danger to human life. A mammal, the orca is an excellent swimmer. Though almost **30 ft** long and weighing up to **11 tons**, it can travel at over **30 mph**.

CATEGORY:
SWIMMING

The competitors are warming up ...

Let's take the time to introduce them ...

✳ TUNA

Sadly, our next competitor is threatened with extinction because of overfishing by humans. What a shame it would be if this ace swimmer were to vanish from the world's oceans forever! We find it in the Atlantic, the Mediterranean and the Black Sea. Measuring up to **8 ft** in length, the tuna can swim at a speed of **45 mph**.

✳ SAILFISH

We find the sailfish in all the world's seas, in both temperate and tropical zones. It is a little less than **7 ft** long. For hunting, it uses the sword that grows from its jawbone. An outstanding swimmer, it can achieve speeds of around **70 mph**.

PARATARSOTOMUS MACROPALPIS

As we close the chapter on record-breaking swimmers, there is one more creature we must mention. Paratarsotomus macropalpis is a mite so tiny that it is not even 0.7 mm long. Nevertheless, it can travel at the amazing speed of 322 body lengths per second. For comparison, imagine a man 6 ft tall running at over 1,200 mph.

RECORD-BREAKING SWIMMERS

1

SAILFISH

70 mph

2

SWORDFISH

60 mph

3

TUNA

45 mph

4

ORCA

30 mph

LONG JUMP

Let's stay in a sporting mood for a while longer. Our next athletics discipline is the long jump. Our competitors are already on the field, warming up. Perhaps you can hear the first one—it's roaring at us.

✳ WHITE-TAILED DEER

There are two deer among our competitors. This one comes from North America. A herbivore, it feeds on grasses and herbs, and is by far a better jumper than its Europe friend. It can leap **45 ft**.

✳ EDIBLE FROG

The edible frog is about 4 in long, and its bright-green body shines in the distance. It feeds on insects and small fish and uses its croak to drive away enemies and intruders. It can jump as far as **3 ft**, which is impressive considering its size. But it is up against some pretty stiff competition today.

✳ BROWN HARE

This 2-foot-long rodent has entered in two disciplines today—we met it first in the 100-meter sprint. Although we don't expect it to match the achievement of the kangaroo or the deer, for its size it can jump quite a distance—over **13 ft**, which is seven times its own length.

CATEGORY:
LONG JUMP

That's a world record!

1   2   3   4   5   6   7   9   10   11   12   13   14

✳ RED KANGAROO

The kangaroo is a marsupial, which means that its young develop in a pouch on the female's belly. About the same height as an adult human, it comes from Australia. Its powerful tail is almost 3 ft in length. It feeds on grasses and flowering plants, and it is a versatile athlete. It can travel at over **35 mph**, and it can jump to a height of **10 ft** and a distance of up to **43 ft**.

✳ SNOW LEOPARD

Our next competitor comes from Asia. With its long, powerful tail that helps it keep its balance in the air, the snow leopard is well qualified to be a long jumper. It is around 2 ft tall and 90 lbs in weight. It lives in the mountains. Though its usual jump is about **20 ft** in length, if it so chooses, it can jump **30 ft**.

✳ RED DEER

Our next horned competitor today comes from Europe. Its build is very similar to that of its North American friend, and it, too, is a herbivore. It is over 6 ft long, weighing 450 lbs and its head is adorned with might antlers. It can jump a distance of **40 ft**. Imagine the power it must have in its legs!

✳ HORSE

The horse has already taken part in the sprint, where it didn't make the victors' podium. But in the discipline known as show jumping, in which the horse and its rider must overcome certain obstacles, it is unbeatable. This time, the horse will be riderless. Without a rider on its back, a horse can jump a distance of **25 ft**.

RECORD-BREAKING LONG JUMPERS

1

WHITE-TAILED DEER
45 ft

2
RED KANGAROO
43 ft

3

RED DEER
40 ft

4

SNOW LEOPARD
30 ft

5

MIKE POWELL
29.36 ft

6

HORSE
25 ft

7

HARE
13 ft

8
EDIBLE FROG
3 ft

✳ THE HUMAN WHO CAN JUMP THE FURTHEST

US athlete Mike Powell is the only human long-jumper ever to have got near the 30-ft mark. His record of **29.36 ft**, achieved in 1991, has still not been bettered. Let's compare the performance of the best human long-jumper with what animals can do.

The art of the long jump doesn't always require a sports field with a landing area. Here are some utterances commonly used by parents. Don't they make you wish you could jump like a white-tailed deer?

"HOP TO IT AND CLEAN YOUR ROOM!"

"JUMP IN AND HELP ME FINISH THE LAUNDRY."

"LOOK BEFORE YOU LEAP!"

We couldn't close the chapter without mentioning a creature that has become practically synonymous with the long jump. It wouldn't stand a chance against our competitors, but its jumping prowess is remarkable nevertheless.

✳ HOUSE FLEA

No one would wish to find one of these parasites—animals that obtain nourishment from another living creature—at home. The house flea sucks blood from its host and can be a carrier of serious diseases. It, too, is a jumper of remarkable powers. Though only 2–3 mm in length, the house flea can jump up to **14 in**—more than one hundred times its body length. For the sake of comparison, if a human could jump as well as a flea, they would have no problem covering a distance of almost 650 ft.

THE WORLD'S SLOWEST ANIMALS

If you think no creature moves more slowly than you when you're doing your household chores, think again. Allow us to introduce some animals that make you on your way home from school with a bad grade in math look like a racehorse approaching the finish line.

To give you a little more thinking time, we'll introduce you first to an animal we have had to disqualify from our competition, as we would need the patience of a meditating monk to measure its speed.

✳ KOALA

The koala, which lives in Australia, is so lazy that it is active for only 5 or 6 hours of the day. It spends three of these sitting in the branches of a eucalyptus tree, eating the leaves. For the 18 hours after that, it probably won't move a muscle, spending most of that time asleep. On waking, ever so slowly it selects another eucalyptus, after which it spends several hours moving toward the tree. Having reached it, it picks through the leaves with the utmost care. When at last it finds one it is prepared to eat, it spends several dozen minutes chewing on it. The koala is the choosiest and laziest animal in the world, by some distance.

Back to our "speedsters." "To move at a snail's pace," they say, meaning as slowly as it is possible to imagine. But the slowest creature of all doesn't look like a slowpoke at all.

DWARF SEAHORSE

About 1 in long, this fish is shaped rather like a horse. It is not much of a swimmer. It prefers to hold on to sea grasses with its tail and wait for its prey. It moves about by wiggling its dorsal fin, at about **5 ft per hour**. Think of the speed at which you perform your household chores and compare it with your speed off the mark when your mom is serving up ice cream. It's similar with the dwarf seahorse—only when food is in sight does it make a rapid movement with its S-shaped neck.

SLOTH

"Sloth" is another word for laziness. So if someone calls you a sloth, they don't think much of your agility. A sloth moves at a speed of around **13 ft per minute**. It spends most of its time wallowing in the tree-tops, coming down to earth only when it feels like it—something you probably understand well. But the sloth comes down only about once a week.

SNAIL

The snail is the second-best slowpoke. There are many snail species—surely you know the one that lives in your garden. Another interesting thing about the snail is that it's hard to tell if it's a boy or a girl. Snails are hermaphrodites, which means that they don't need a member of the opposite sex to reproduce. So how fast is this "sprinter"? Well, it can move at an impressive **16 ft per hour.**

TORTOISE

We're sure you know the joke about the zookeeper who was so terribly slow that before he managed to close the gate of the tortoise enclosure, all the tortoises escaped. That zookeeper must have been a real slacker, because most tortoises travel at about twice the speed of a sloth. In an hour, a tortoise will get no further than **a quarter-mile**.

❋ DOMESTIC DUCK

The quickest of the slowpokes is the duck, although it isn't much of a mover either. The duck can cover about **one-third of a mile in an hour**. But as its job is to provide feathers and eggs, humans are pleased with its slowness.

SLOWPOKES GO TO SCHOOL

Now you know the speeds of the world's slowest animals. Imagine that you are one of them. How long would it take you to get to school if it was **1 mile** away from your home?

4 HOURS

At tortoise speed, it would take you 4 hours to reach a school 1 mile away.

7 HOURS

At sloth speed, the walk to school would take you nearly 7 hours.

14 DAYS

At a snail's pace, it would take you 330 hours to crawl to your physics class—that's 2 weeks. You would have lots of time to finish your homework on the way.

44 DAYS

How about this?! If your speed was equal to that of the dwarf seahorse, your walk to school would take 1,056 hours—which is 44 days, or 6 weeks. Over 1 month to get to school, and over 1 month to get home again. Like that, over the whole school year you would get to go to school a maximum of four times before the holidays arrived. What a great life a dwarf seahorse must have!

THE WORLD'S STRONGEST ANIMALS

All of us are sometimes required to lift something. The least fit among us break into a sweat when picking up a shopping bag. But well-trained athletes can lift dozens of pounds without batting an eyelid. Weightlifters are athletes who specialize in heavy lifting. The current world record in the discipline where the athlete lifts the weight over his head is 582 lbs. The record in the deadlift, where the athlete lifts a barbell to the level of the hips, is 1,104 lbs. Let's look at feats of strength achieved by animals.

By measuring weightlifting ability against body weight, we come up with some interesting animal record holders.

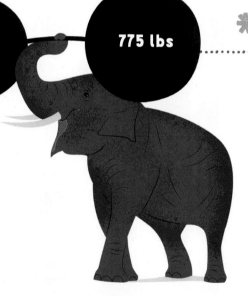

775 lbs

✳ ELEPHANT

The elephant is well capable of lifting a very heavy load. Considering its size, however, this is hardly surprising. The Indian elephant is almost 10 ft high and weighs about 5.5 tons. Its 6-foot-long trunk alone can lift up to **775 lbs**; with its body, it can lift **several tons**. If we consider the weight of the load only, the elephant is the world's strongest animal.

1.65 tons

✳ GORILLA

The gorilla may be enormously strong, but it is a peaceful creature. Depending on the species, it is between 5 and 5.5 ft tall, and it weighs about **330 lbs**. The remarkable thing is, it can lift a weight **10 times greater** than its own—up to 1.65 tons! Turning over your car would be child's play for a gorilla. Sadly, gorilla species are critically endangered.

30 lbs

✳ GOLDEN EAGLE

A Goliath among birds, its wingspan is around 6.5 ft. Although it feeds mainly on small animals, it is capable of hunting down a young deer. Its claws can carry away prey that weigh **30 lbs**. As the eagle itself weighs only about 6 lbs, this means it can lift **five times its own weight**.

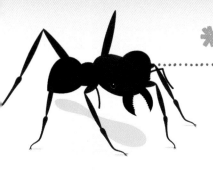

ANTS OF THE ATTA GENUS

If we want to tell someone they are weak, we may compare them to an ant. But this is a feeble comparison: for instance, ants of the Atta genus can lift up to **50 times their own weight**. To match the feat, a comparably strong human would have to lift 8,250 lbs.

TAURUS SCARAB

The true record holder by lifting capacity in relation to its own weight is another beetle. We declare the taurus scarab the world's strongest animal! It may be only 1 cm in length, but it can lift an incredible **1,140 times its own weight**.

RHINOCEROS BEETLE

An inhabitant of Malaysia, this beetle can lift **850 times its own weight**. A human of average weight but comparable strength would be able to lift almost 70 tons.

Compared to the taurus scarab, a comparably strong human would be able to lift above their head one of the lighter whales, which weigh around 100 tons.

RECORD-BREAKING POWERHOUSES

1. ELEPHANT — **several tons**
2. GORILLA — **1.65 tons**
3. EAGLE — **30 lbs**

1. TAURUS SCARAB — **1,140 times more**
2. RHINOCEROS BEETLE — **850 times more**
3. ATTA ANT — **50 times more**

850 times more

1,140 times more

50 times more

THE WORLD'S LARGEST ANIMALS

Having put animal strength to the test, let's now turn to the bodily dimensions of animal record holders. Let's see which animals are the largest in their group. We begin with the very largest creature alive on our planet.

❊ BLUE WHALE

The blue whale holds two records. Not only is it the largest animal currently alive on Earth, it is also the heaviest creature of all time. It grows to be over **100 ft** in length—as long as two trucks parked back to front. Its weight reaches an incredible **210 tons**—equivalent to a load that would fill almost 8 trucks. It can live to be over 80 years old. It lives in nearly all the world's oceans.

ELEPHANT RECORDS

With over 40,000 muscles, an elephant's trunk serves as a very precise instrument. What's more, an elephant has an excellent memory and is one of few animals that can recognize itself in a mirror.

❊ AFRICAN ELEPHANT

The African elephant is the largest terrestrial animal. It can grow to be **13 ft** tall and commonly weighs around **6.5 tons** (although the weight of the heaviest individual was measured at around **11 tons**). Straight after birth, an elephant calf weighs 220 lbs. An elephant's life span is between 70 and 90 years.

SPERM WHALE RECORDS

Largest toothed animal in the world. Mammal that dives deepest (over 1 mile). Has the largest brain (weight: 15 lbs) of all inhabitants of Earth.

SPERM WHALE

Resident in the world's oceans, the sperm whale has a large head and is almost **65 ft** long. It weighs around **55 tons,** lives for up to 80 years and is the holder of several world records.

MASAI GIRAFFE

The world's tallest animal, this species of giraffe lives in east Africa. It is up to **20 ft** tall and weighs over a ton. About half of its height is accounted for by its **10-foot-long neck**. Despite its great length, a giraffe's neck has only 7 vertebrae—the same number as a human's. Thanks to this neck, the giraffe can nibble on leaves in the treetops.

GIANT SIPHONOPHORE

An inhabitant of the ocean deep, this fascinating creature is a record holder, too: its body is up to **165 ft long**—that's the length of at least 10 passenger cars parked back to front in a line. A cnidarian, the siphonophore uses light emitted by its body to attract its prey, which it kills with its venomous stinging cells.

POLAR BEAR

The largest predatory mammal in the world that stands on its hind legs, the polar bear is over **10 ft** tall and weighs around **1,500 lbs**. Yet a polar bear cub weighs only 1 lb at birth. The polar bear lives on ice floes and land beyond the Arctic Circle. A hunter of small animals, seals and walruses, it also represents a danger to humans. It is such a strong swimmer that it can cover **hundreds of miles** in the water.

SIBERIAN TIGER

Being slightly larger than the lion, it is the largest feline predator alive today. Its typical body length is over **6 ft**, to which is added a 3-foot-long tail. The male weighs over **440 lbs**. Unlike the lion, the Siberian tiger lives a solitary life. It preys on wild pigs, deer and other, smaller mammals. Tigers are found in India, Russia, Indonesia, Malaysia and a few other places in the world.

LION

The magnificent lion may not be the very largest feline predator, but it is considered by all to be the king of the animals. An adult lion weighs around **400 lbs** and is almost **6 ft** long. Most lions live in Africa and a small area of India. The lion could be a record holder in doing nothing, as it rests for up to 20 hours a day.

ANTEATER RECORDS

Although the anteater is not one of the world's largest animals, it holds one record for sure. Measuring up to 2 ft, its tongue is longer than that of any other creature.

EMPEROR SCORPION

I hope you're not afraid of scorpions, because we're about to introduce you to the very biggest of them. It lives in Africa and may grow to be **8 in** long. How horrible it would be to find such an animal in your bed! Yet a bite from an emperor scorpion will cause nothing worse than itching, the effects of which will soon wear off. Other kinds of scorpions are far more dangerous, however.

BLUE WILDEBEEST

About 6 ft long, the wildebeest forms the largest herds. These herds comprise **tens of thousands of individuals**.

GIANT SQUID

We know very little about this deep-ocean-dwelling cephalopod, and there are not many photographs of it. But we know for sure that it is one of our planet's largest creatures—the length of the body and eight arms of the largest individual seen was **60 ft**.

SQUID RECORDS

The squid is as high as a 6-story building. With a diameter of about 1 ft, its eye is the largest in the animal kingdom—about the same size as a human head.

19

WHAT ABOUT THE LITTLE ONES?

That's quite enough of the giants. After all, the very smallest also have a right to life. Let's look now at creatures that haven't grown much. If you happen to be in their vicinity, be careful not to tread on them. They have their records, too, you know—concerning how small they are.

❋ ETRUSCAN SHREW

At only **2 grams** (the weight of less than half a bag of sugar), it is the world's smallest mammal in terms of body weight. And as its body is only about **1.5 in** long, it could fit inside a matchbox comfortably. This shrew has a life span of about one year. We find it in Europe, Africa and certain parts of Asia.

RECORDS HELD BY THE ETRUSCAN SHREW

By mass, the smallest known mammal. Though tiny, it can jump a distance of 8 in.

❋ BUMBLEBEE BAT

This bat is the world's smallest mammal in terms of body size; at only **1 in** long, it is not much bigger than a human fingernail. It lives in Thailand and Burma.

RECORD HELD BY THE EASTERN PYGMY POSSUM

It can sleep for over a year.

❋ EASTERN PYGMY POSSUM

It lives in Australia and Tasmania, weighs about **25 grams** and is a little less than **4 in** long. Although tiny, in terms of body size it is not the very smallest mammal. It holds a different interesting record, however. To save energy from the food its body has taken in, it falls into a very long sleep.

MOST BEAUTIFUL BABY ANIMALS

The very smallest are lovely, aren't they? So let's stay with little cuties for a while. These may not be the world's smallest, but for many readers they are the most beautiful. So here they are—the world's cutest baby animals.

✳ BABY GORILLA

At birth, a gorilla weighs about **5 lbs**. Its mother takes care of it until it is about **3 years old.** Gorillas are brought up by their parents in a similar way to humans, and they are highly intelligent. Some gorillas kept in a zoo can communicate in sign language. The western gorilla can live up to 60 years.

✳ BABY FENNEC

This lovely pointy-eared creature is most active at night, as it prefers a lower air temperature. It reaches adulthood at around **9 months** of age.

✳ GREY MOUSE LEMUR

The grey mouse lemur is one of the world's smallest primates—in adulthood it is only about **4 in** long. It lives in Madagascar and gives birth to two or three young at a time. Its baby weighs only **6 grams**.

✳ BABY MEERKAT

Born blind, it begins to see after about **14 days**. Young are cared for by the whole meerkat colony, comprising up to **30 individuals**.

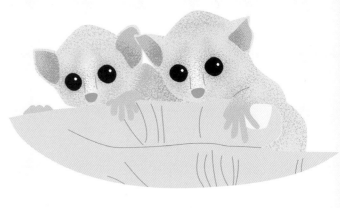

✳ LION CUB

Lions give birth to between one and four cubs at a time. When these cubs grow up, the leader of the pack drives them away; lions must make their own way in life.

✳ BABY GOLDEN EAGLE

The female lays two eggs, which she heats with her body for **45 days** before the eggs hatch and lovely, snow-white chicks emerge. Sadly, in many cases only the stronger sibling survives; in the fight for food, the weaker is pushed from the nest by the stronger. The golden eagle has a life span of about **25 years**.

✳ BABY EMPEROR PENGUIN

The female presents one of her eggs to the male, who keeps it warm between his legs for a period of 64 days. An adult emperor penguin can dive to a depth of over **1,600 ft** and stay underwater for **30 minutes**. Some penguins can achieve an underwater speed of **25 mph**. Where they live, the temperature can drop to **-40°F**, so it's not surprising they have the densest feathers of all birds.

✳ BABY GIRAFFE

About **6 ft** tall, a new-born giraffe can stand within **20 minutes** of its birth. To that point, it has grown in the body of the giraffe mom for up to **460 days**.

✳ BABY ELEPHANT

An unborn elephant grows inside its mother for 22 months. At birth, it is over **3 ft** tall and weighs around **220 lbs**. The female feeds her calf for 2 years, and she will do all she can to protect it from danger. Elephants live for about **70 years**.

THE UGLIEST ANIMALS

What a fascinating place our world is! It contains animals large and small, animals fast and slow, animals that weigh tons and animals that weigh but a few grams. Alongside the magnificent creatures, however, we find some that are less than beautiful. But these, too, have a place in the bizarre animal world. Let's look at them now.

✳ AYE-AYE

It has ears like a bat's, lives in Madagascar and is the world's **largest nocturnal prosimian**. Its long fingers end in nails. It uses its longest, middle finger to pick out its food—larvae from tree bark, the milk of the coconut and the contents of birds' eggs.

✳ BLOBFISH

This slimy fish is the **winner of the World's Ugliest Animal competition**. Too lazy to hunt for food, it just lies on the seabed with its mouth open, swallowing up whatever comes its way.

✳ PROBOSCIS MONKEY

This monkey with a cucumber-shaped nose lives on the island of Borneo. You wouldn't be the first to laugh at its appearance. The nose of the male is **4 in** long. For comparison, if the human nose and body were in the same proportion, the nose would be almost **1 foot long**.

✳ PHILIPPINE TARSIER

This small, large-eyed animal comes from the rainforests of the Philippines. Active at night, it is about the same size as the human palm. It weighs about **100 grams** and can jump a distance of **16 ft**.

UAKARI

The uakari is another monkey that would stand no chance in a beauty contest. It is slightly over **20 in** long and immediately recognized by its red face. The darker the uakari's face, the healthier it is. Indeed, the male chooses a mate for the color of her face.

GOBLIN SHARK

The strange shark with a bayonet on its head is the goblin. It is a living fossil, which means that its appearance hasn't changed for tens of millions of years.

AARDVARK

Another of the many animals passed over when beauty was being handed out. The front of its head looks like a pig's snout, and its hefty, **3-foot-long** body is practically bald. It lives in Africa, feeding on ants and termites.

PLATYPUS

The platypus is a very odd-looking, egg-laying mammal. It has a broad, flat tail and the front of its head looks like a duck's. It lives only in eastern Australia. Its body temperature is only **90°F**.

NAKED MOLE-RAT

Native to Africa, this odd rodent is exceptional for being born in a nest shared by **300 other individuals** of its species. Young are cared for in the group. It uses its large, protruding teeth to dig out a labyrinth of corridors underground, in which everything—including a precisely demarcated pantry, bedroom and toilet—has its place. The mole-rat is almost blind.

WESTERN LONG-BEAKED ECHIDNA

We find another oddity of the animal world on the island of New Guinea. The western long-beaked echidna looks a bit like a hedgehog with a bird's beak. A critically endangered nocturnal creature, it feeds on insects. As it is a mammal, its young are nourished on mother's milk. But unlike most other mammals, which give birth to live young, the echidna lays eggs from which its offspring hatch.

AMAZONIAN MANATEE

The Amazonian manatee lives in the Amazon Basin, is **8 ft long** and weighs **660 lbs**. It spends half the day sleeping underwater. When it sleeps, half of its brain remains active, allowing it to come to the surface and breathe.

AXOLOTL

The larva of the axolotl can grow to be **14 in** long. Native to the lakes of Mexico, if it happens to lose a limb, it can generate a new one.

PIG-NOSED TURTLE

This species of turtle is easily recognized by its nose, which ends in a snout like a pig's. Females lay up to **30 eggs** in hollows in the sand of the riverbank. It lives in Australia and on the island of New Guinea.

DESERT WARTHOG

This strange wild pig lives in Africa. It is about **30 in** tall and **5 ft** long, and it weighs **330 lbs**. Its face is adorned by three pairs of warts. The tusks protruding from its upper jaw can be **2 ft** long. A second pair of tusks growing from the lower jaw are about half that length.

THE MOST DANGEROUS ANIMALS

Over the next few pages, we will look at animals you should be very wary of. These animals are considered to pose the greatest danger to human life. Reasons for this danger include a tendency to attack, to act in self-defense or to rely on deadly venom.

☀ ELEPHANT

Most of the time, the world's largest animal is very peaceful. When angered or—in the case of the female—protecting its young, however, the elephant can get really upset. When it does, we must get out of its way immediately.

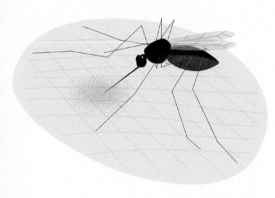

☀ MOSQUITO

How strange it is that this small creature should top the list of the world's most dangerous animals! It is said to cause the deaths of over **1 million** people a year. This is because it is a carrier of infectious diseases, such as malaria, West Nile virus and yellow fever.

☀ AFRICAN BUFFALO

In Africa, the buffalo is known as "the Black Death." It is one of Africa's five most dangerous animals. Extremely persistent, it can pursue its prey for many miles, reaching speeds of **35 mph**.

SHARK

The shark can smell a single drop of blood from a quarter of a mile away. There are many shark species, only a few of which are a threat to humans. The most dangerous of all is the great white shark, which is around **16 ft** in length and **2,200 lbs** in weight. Hundreds of attacks on humans by white sharks have been recorded.

JELLYFISH

The shark is not the only dangerous animal in the sea—far from it. Jellyfish are beautiful and magical to look at. But there are species of jellyfish (notably the box jellyfish and the Portuguese man-of-war) whose tentacles are armed with venomous cells. If stung by such a jellyfish, a human will not survive without medical treatment.

LION

Sharp claws and teeth, an ability to run at very high speed, the hunter's instinct of a meat-loving predator—all this makes the lion very dangerous to the human. Although lions rarely attack humans, such cases happen, so we must take great care around them.

ATTACK ON A RAILWAY LINE

Late in the 19th century, two cannibalistic lions appeared on a railway line in Kenya. By the time they were shot, over 100 people were dead.

SNAKE

Venomous snakes are very dangerous for humans, too, of course. The venom of some may cause humans to suffer painful cramps. Other snakes are so venomous that their bite can kill a human within minutes. The most dangerous snakes include the **Indian cobra** and the **mamba**. However, humans rarely come in contact with venomous snakes, and non-venomous species are not only harmless but beneficial to our ecosystem.

CROCODILE

A reptile, the crocodile will eat flesh of any kind. In areas where crocodiles live, humans must always take great care. The crocodile inspires respect by its size alone: the saltwater crocodile can grow to a length of **23 ft**, and it weighs a **full ton**. No surprise, then, that it is a merciless killer. It lies in wait for its prey in the water, from which it mounts a lightning-fast attack.

CONE SNAIL

Don't be deceived by the appearance of this sea snail with a lovely shell. It can grow to be **4 in** long. The toxins in its sting can kill other creatures, including humans.

A RUNNING HIPPO

On land, a hippopotamus can reach a speed of 18 mph.

SCORPION

There are many species of scorpion, and all of them are venomous. They use their venom to paralyse their prey. Not every scorpion sting represents a threat to humans, however; only a few species (e.g., the **deathstalker** and **Hemiscorpius**) have a venom that can kill a human.

BROWN BEAR

Although the brown bear is nowhere near the top of the danger rankings, if it attacks a human it can inflict very serious injury. In places where bears live, we must behave with extreme caution and respect certain rules; we should never leave the marked path or make a noise that could scare a bear, for instance. A person under attack from a bear should curl up and protect their head.

HIPPOPOTAMUS

Africa's most dangerous mammal, the hippopotamus is responsible for many human deaths each year. Its jaw-grip is one of the most powerful of all animals. It may not look like much of a runner, but it can move extremely fast. Seemingly pudgy and peaceful, in fact it is a merciless killer and vicious defender of its territory.

LONGEST-LIVING ANIMALS

The average life span of the human is a little less than 80 years; only occasionally do we meet a person who has lived to be over 100. The longest-lived human died at 114 years of age. But some of our planet's creatures go way beyond that.

THE INDIAN ELEPHANT AND THE BOWHEAD WHALE

These are the mammals with the longest life span. The oldest known bowhead whale lived for 211 years.

KOI

The Japanese keep carp for decoration. The koi commonly lives for about **50 years**, but there is one known case of a koi living **226 years**.

GIANT TORTOISE

This tortoise weighs 440 lbs. It lives in the Seychelles, commonly for **160 years**. A tortoise called Adwaita, which was taken by British sailors from its native islands to Calcutta Zoo, lived to the age of **255 years**.

THE IMMORTAL JELLYFISH

For its ability to reverse its life cycle in an emergency, the creature with the Latin name Turritopsis dohrnii is known as "the immortal jellyfish." Imagine if a human in distress could return to their childhood! It sounds incredible, but this is exactly what this jellyfish can do.

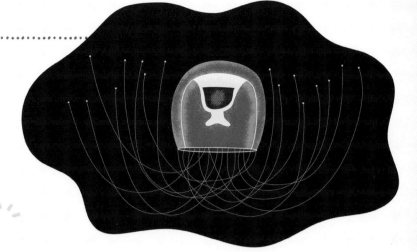

MAYFLY

Now let's look at the other end of the life-span scale. The winged insect known as the mayfly lives for a record short time—only **1–3 days**.

CINACHYRA ANTARCTICA

The species of sponge Cinachyra antarctica lives in the cold seas of the continent it is named for. It is known to have lived for **1,550 years**.

OCEAN QUAHOG

This species of marine bivalve lives in the Atlantic Ocean for hundreds of years. The oldest individual specimen lived **507 years**.

WORLD-RECORD TRAVELERS

✳ ARCTIC TERN

This bird is the record holder for length of migratory flight. Having nested in North America, it spends the winter in Antarctica. This means that it makes the long journey **from pole to pole** twice a year.

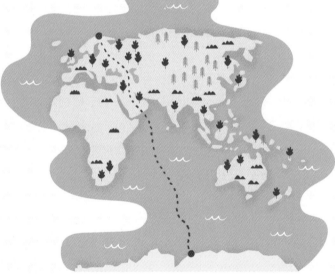

✳ WOLVERINE

The largest of the Mustelids is a very competent tourist. It is almost 3 ft long and weighs up to 55 lbs. Its territory is huge. When on its travels, it can cover **hundreds of miles** in a single month.